Clown Fish

Curious Kids Press

Please note:All Rights Reserved. No part of this publication may be reproduced in any form or by any means, including scanning, photocopying, or otherwise without prior written permission of the copyright holder. Copyright © 2014

Clownfish

The Clownfish is very cool. It is also known as the Anemonefish; we will discover why later on in this book. There are 28 species of the Clownfish. The most common one is orange with white markings. What makes this little fish so popular? Read on to discover many cool facts about this popular fish. In this book we will discover all sorts of new and interesting things. So sit back and be prepared to be wowed. Read on….

Where in the World?

Did you know the Clownfish can be found in many different regions? It likes to hang out in the coral reefs. These can be found in the Indian and Pacific Oceans. Some Clownfish live as far north as the Red Sea. Here the Clownfish can be found in the Great Barrier Reef. This is on the Australian Coast.

The Most Famous Clown Fish

Did you know the Clownfish is famous? Who is this cute character? His name is Nemo, from the Finding Nemo movie. This little fish had an awesome adventure with all his friends in the ocean. If you want your very own Clownfish as a pet, read on to discover what you will need to do.

The Body of a Clown Fish

Did you know the Clownfish comes in different colors? The biggest species of Clownfish can measure up to 7.1 inches long (18 centimetres). The smallest Clownfish is around 3.9 inches long (10 centimetres). Clownfish come in many different colors including orange or black and white, pink and even ones with blue on them.

What a Clown Fish Eats

Did you know the Clownfish is an omnivore? This means it will eat both plants and meat. In the warm summer months, the Clown fish eats small shrimp, zooplankton and other animal matter. In the cold winter months, this fish will eat plant matter like algae. This fish also has a special way of getting its food.

Clown Fish are Helpers

Did you know the Clownfish and anemones are friends? This is very strange since anemones have hundreds of poisonous tentacles. Plus, they eat fish. But not the Clownfish. The anemone likes the Clownfish because it eats its dead tentacles. The Clownfish also protects the anemone from predators. Read on to find out how the Clownfish can do this.

The Clown Fish Has a Special Ability

Did you know the Clownfish has a special dance it does? This fish really is a clown. It does a funky dance around the tentacles of the anemone to avoid its sting. However, the Clownfish does allow some of the poisonous tentacles to graze its skin. By doing this over and over, the Clownfish becomes immune to the toxins.

Enemies of the Clown Fish

Did you know humans are a big threat to the Clownfish? The Clown fish is caught by people to put into pet stores for sale. This is very stressful on the Clownfish. This fish also has lots of natural predators like eels, sharks and bigger fish. But remember the anemone? The Clownfish hides in this poisonous creature to escape from its natural predators.

Clown Fish Mom and Dad

Did you know the girl Clown fish lays hundreds and even thousands of eggs? Mom Clownfish lays her eggs on a flat surface. But this is always close to her friend the anemone. The sting of the anemone helps keep the eggs safe. Mom will lay her eggs when their is a full moon in the sky. Dad Clownfish then guards the eggs.

Baby Clown Fish

Did you know baby Clown fish hatches from their eggs a week after being laid? All the baby Clownfish are born boys. When breeding season happens, one of the boy Clownfish will turn female. It will breed with one of the male Clownfish living in the same sea anemone. This is really weird!

Clown Fish as Pets

Did you know you can keep a Clownfish as a pet? Clownfish can be found in some pet stores. This pet needs to have a very special aquarium. The water must always be warm. It is also a saltwater fish. Clownfish cannot live in a bowl, like a goldfish. This fish needs special care to live a happy life.

Life of a Clown Fish

Did you know the Clownfish can live a long time? Some Clownfish have been known to live as long as 25 years in aquariums. However, no one really knows how long this fish can live in the wild. The Clown fish spends most of its time in and around the anemone. They are BFF's!

The Pink Skunk Clownfish

Did you know this Clownfish is pink in color? It got its name from the white stripe running along its back. This fish can grow up to 4 inches long (10 centimeters). In the wild it can be found in the Eastern Indian Ocean and the Western Pacific Ocean. It can also live close to Australia.

Saddle-Back Clownfish

Did you know this fish is black and white? The Saddle-Back Clownfish is known for its unique white saddle-pattern on its back. It is found in the Eastern Indian ocean and the Western Pacific. This cool fish swims up and down in a funky style. It too lives with its anemone friend.

Tomato Clownfish

Did you know this Clownfish is the color of a tomato? Male Tomato Clownfish have a red body with a single white stripe around its head. Young Tomato Clownfish have 2 to 3 white bars. The female is bigger and she has a blackish color on her sides. Her belly, front and snout have white on it.

Quiz

Question 1: How many species of the Clownfish are there?

Answer 1: About 28

Question 2: Who is the most famous Clownfish?

Answer 2: *Nemo*

Question 3: What is the Clownfish a helper to?

Answer 3: The sea anemone

Question 4: What special ability does the Clownfish have?

Answer 4: : It is immune to the anemone's toxins

Question 5: How many eggs does the mom Clownfish have?

Answer 5: Hundreds to thousands at one time

Thank you for checking out another title from Curious Kids Press! Make sure to search "Curious Kids Press" on Amazon.com for many other great books.

CPSIA information can be obtained at www.ICGtesting.com
Printed in the USA
LVIW01n1432250116
472163LV00026B/164